ER POWELL M
Powell, Marie, 1958-
Get wet!

Get Wet!

by Marie Powell

illustrated by Amy Cartwright

amicus
readers

Ideas for Parents and Teachers

Amicus Readers let children practice reading at early reading levels. Familiar words and concepts with close illustration-text matches support early readers.

Before Reading

- Discuss the cover illustration with the child. What does it tell him?
- Ask the child to predict what she will learn in the book.

Read the Book

- "Walk" through the book and look at the illustrations. Let the child ask questions.
- Point out the colored words. Ask the child what is the same about them (spelling, ending sound).
- Read the book to the child, or have the child read to you.

After Reading

- Use the word family list at the end of the book to review the text.
- Prompt the child to make connections. Ask: *What other words end with -et?*

Amicus Readers are published by Amicus
P.O. Box 1329, Mankato, MN 56002
www.amicuspublishing.us

Illustrations by Amy Cartwright

Produced for Amicus by The Peterson Publishing Company and Red Line Editorial.

Editor Jenna Gleisner
Designer Craig Hinton
Printed in the United States of America
Mankato, MN
1-2014
PA10001
10 9 8 7 6 5 4 3 2 1

Library of Congress Cataloging-in-Publication Data
Powell, Marie, 1958-
  Get wet! / Marie Powell.
     pages cm. -- (Word families)
  Audience: Age 6.
  K to Grade 3.
  ISBN 978-1-60753-581-2 (hardcover) --
  ISBN 978-1-60753-647-5 (pdf ebook)
  1. Reading--Phonetic method. 2. Readers (Primary) I. Title.
LB1573.3.P6936 2014
372.465--dc23
                    2013043998

My name is **Bret**. Today **Chet** and I are at the pool.

4

Chet swims as fast as a rocket. But I am not ready yet.

I let my toes touch the water. It feels cold and wet.

"Set your legs over the edge. Go ahead and **get wet!**" Chet says.

8

Now I **let** my feet dangle in the water.

"Let me get used to it,"
I say.

Chet says, "Do not fret,
Bret. I will not splash you."

Then I forget about my fear.

"Are you ready yet?" asks Chet.

"You bet!" I say.

I am glad I met Chet at the pool today.
"Time to get wet!" I say.
Splash!

Word Family: -et

Word families are groups of words that rhyme and are spelled the same.

Here are the -et words in this book:

bet	let
Bret	met
Chet	rocket
forget	set
fret	wet
get	yet

Can you spell any other words with -et?